STEP-UP
HISTORY

How did your locality change in Victorian times?

Jill Barber

Evans

Published by Evans Brothers Limited
2A Portman Mansions
Chiltern Street
London W1U 6NR

© Evans Brothers Limited 2006

Produced for Evans Brothers Limited by
White-Thomson Publishing Ltd,
Bridgewater Business Centre,
210 High Street,
Lewes, East Sussex BN7 2NH

Printed in China by New Era Printing Co. Ltd .

Project manager: Ruth Nason

Designer: Helen Nelson, Jet the Dog

Series consultant: Rosie-Turner Bisset, Reader
in Education and Director of Learning and
Teaching, Faculty of Education, University
of Middlesex

British Library Cataloguing in Publication Data
Barber, Jill

How did your locality change in Victorian times?
- (Step-up history)
1. Great Britain - Social conditions - 19th century
- Juvenile literature
2. Great Britain - History - Victoria, 1837-1901 -
Juvenile literature
I. Title
941'.081

ISBN-13: 9780237531485
ISBN-10: 0237531488

Picture acknowledgements:

Every effort has been made to trace copyright
holders. If any have been omitted from this list, the
Publishers will correct this at reprint.

Peter Barber: pages 4, 16t, 17t, 17c, 20, 21, 22,
23t, 23br, 24, 25bl, 25br; Borough Museum and
Art Gallery, Newcastle-under-Lyme: page 12b;
Camden Local Studies and Archives Centre: cover
(centre) and pages 11, 17b; City of Westminster
Archives Centre: page 15; Coors Visitor Centre &
Museum of Brewing Collection, Burton on Trent:
page 13t; © English Heritage: pages 12t, 25t;
Hertfordshire Archives and Local Studies: pages
5bl, 5r (David Dent), 7c, 13c, 13b, 18b, 27t, 27b;
Knowsley Library Service: page 9t, 9b; Mary Evans
Picture Library: pages 16b, 19l; Karen Noble: page
23bl; Science and Society Picture Library: page 10;
Alan Smith: page 1; Staffordshire Arts and Museum
Service: pages 14t, 14b, 19r; The National
Archives: pages 6, 7t; Topfoto: page 18t (©
University of York); Tring and District Local History
and Museum Society/the Grace Collection: page
5tl.

Thanks also to Hertfordshire Archives and Local
Studies for the use of documents on pages 10, 11.

Contents

Finding out about the Victorians

The Victorians were people who lived in Britain during the reign of Queen Victoria (1837-1901). This was a time of great change. Industry grew and Britain became one of the most wealthy and powerful countries in the world. The changes affected people's lives throughout the country.

SMETHWICK LOCAL HISTORY SOCIETY

Site of the
THREE SHIRES OAK

An ancient marker
of the boundaries of
Staffordshire, Worcestershire
and Shropshire
uprooted circa 1900

2000

◀ *Why do you think this ancient oak tree was uprooted? You will find out if you are right on page 26.*

Collecting clues

One good way to find out about your locality in Victorian times is to walk around the area looking at the buildings. You might find clues like those in the photographs here.

CORN EXCHANGE
CONSTRUCTED BY PUBLIC SUBSCRIPTION
HENRY DAY ESQ BAILIFF

GEORGE LOW   A:D : 1857   WILLIAM SEAR
ARCHITECT   BUILDER

MR GOSLING'S HOMES
FOR AGED WOMEN.
FOUNDED 1896

▲
▶ *Look for buildings in your locality that date from Victorian times.*

Finding the evidence

You can also look at documents written in Victorian times.

- Census returns show who lived in each house.
- Reports by inspectors and medical officers describe what Victorian towns were like, especially the toilets!
- Newspapers include local events.
- Trade and street directories tell us about shops, industries, transport, schools and churches.
- Letters and diaries reveal what happened to people, and what they thought about it.
- Maps and plans give a picture of what was on the ground.

Picturing the past

The earliest photographs of your area probably date from the 1860s or 1870s. To see what places looked like in early Victorian times we have to rely on artists' impressions, in drawings and paintings.

Using evidence

Visit your local studies library, archive or museum to find sources for your area in Victorian times. Always remember to ask questions to discover the stories the sources have to tell.

◀ *This photograph is intriguing. Are the people waiting for something? Can you tell if the women are poor or rich? What are they doing? Where are they standing? What are they looking at? Who is watching them? Perhaps you could write a caption.*

▼ *Advertisements in local newspapers tell us about life in Victorian times. This one from 1884 shows the type of lamps people used before they had electricity in their homes.*

The BURGLAR'S HORROR.
CLARKE'S PATENT
PYRAMID NIGHT LAMPS
1s. EACH, SOLD EVERYWHERE.

CAUTION.—TO PREVENT BURGLARIES.

A Pyramid Night Light should be lighted in a front and back room of every house, as soon as it is dark. Burglaries are more frequently perpetrated before bedtime than after. Housebreakers have the greatest dread of a light. The police recommend a Night Light as the best safeguard. Almost all burglaries may be prevented, and much *valuable property saved*, if this simple and inexpensive plan is adopted. The Pyramid Night Lights are much larger and give *three times the light* of the common night lights, and are therefore particularly adapted for this purpose.

PATENT PYRAMID NIGHT LIGHT WORKS,
CHILD'S-HILL, LONDON, N.W.

▲ *Postcards became very popular in the 1890s. You can find them for most villages and streets. As roads improved, people enjoyed cycling. At first it was only for men. The Victorians did not think it was 'lady-like'. In the late 1890s women also began to ride bicycles, in spite of their long skirts.*

Who lived here?

Would you like to know who lived in your house, street, town or village in Victorian times? You can find out from census returns. A census is taken every ten years.

The government first decided to find out how many people there were in the country in 1801. A visit was made to every house, to count who was there on one particular night. Barns and boats were checked to make sure that no one was left out. The information collected was written into books called census returns. People's names were first recorded in 1841.

What can the census tell us?

On the right is a page from the 1841 census returns for Hertford. Find the address Butcherley Green in the left-hand column. The census gives the names of the people in each house. You can also find out people's ages, and the jobs they did.

You can compare the information in different census years to find out how life changed. From 1851, census returns show how people were related and where they were born.

▲ Reading Victorian handwriting is like doing a puzzle. Which names can you read? 'Do' or 'ditto' means the same as the name above. This census page shows that in Butcherley Green in 1841 there was a basket woman, a wheelwright, a chimney sweep and an agricultural labourer.

▶ *The 1891 census lists 11 people in the Sterne family.*

Administrative County of Hertfordshire							The undermentioned Houses are situate within the Boundaries of the								Page 37	

(census form for 246 Charles Street, Berkhamsted)

No. of Schedule	ROAD, STREET, &c., and No. or NAME of HOUSE	HOUSES			NAME and Surname of each Person	RELATION to Head of Family	CONDITION as to Marriage	AGE last Birthday of		PROFESSION or OCCUPATION	Employer	Employed	Neither Employer nor Employed	WHERE BORN	If (1) Deaf-and-Dumb (2) Blind (3) Lunatic, Imbecile or Idiot
246	Charles Street	1			Harry Sterne	Head	M	39		Brushmaker	X			Herts Berkhamsted	
					Emma Sterne	Wife	M		37					Bucks Aylesbury	
					Alice Sterne	Daur	S		18	Brushmaker		X		Herts Berkhamsted	
					Sarah Sterne	Daur	S		16	Do		X		Do Do	
					Frank Sterne	Son		13		Scholar				Lancashire Aston Under Lyne	
					Harry Sterne	Son		11		Do				Fenny Stratford Bucks	
					Eliza Sterne	Daur			8	Do				Do Do	
					George Sterne	Son		6		Do				Herts Berkhamsted	
					Fred Sterne	Son		5		Do				Do Do	
					Arthur Sterne	Son		4		Do				Do Do	
					Charles Sterne	Son		2						Do Do	

▶ *This photograph of Harry and Emma Sterne and their children was taken in 1887. Why is Charles missing from the picture? See if you can use the census to work out the names of the children in the photograph.*

▼ *In this cartoon the census enumerator has come to collect the census form. There are so many people in the family that the father cannot remember all their names. The average Victorian family had five or six children.*

Taking a census

Design a census form. What questions will you ask? Fill in the form for your own house or family. How do you know the information is right? Can you think of any reasons why people might sometimes not want to tell the truth?

Doing a people count

Some dramatic changes took place in the 64 years of Queen Victoria's reign. More than twice as many people lived in Britain at the end of her reign than at the beginning.

By counting people in census returns in different ways, we can investigate some of the changes that took place in a locality between 1841 and 1901. We can explore:

- how many people lived there
- how they moved around
- what type of jobs they did.

Moving about

In early Victorian times most people lived in the same place for all their life. As time went on, people moved about more. They moved to towns to find work. Some village populations decreased as towns grew. Find out what happened in your area.

In the late 1840s, many people left Ireland to escape a famine. Irish men who came to Britain helped to build the railways.

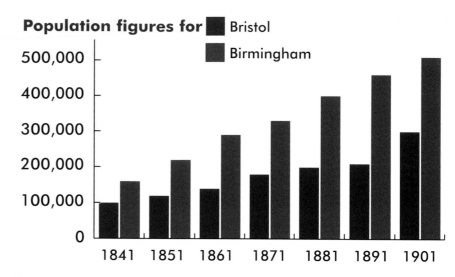

Population figures for ■ Bristol ■ Birmingham

▲ Towns and cities, such as Birmingham and Bristol, grew in Victorian times. Birmingham became the second largest city in Britain, after London. In which decade did Bristol's population grow most?

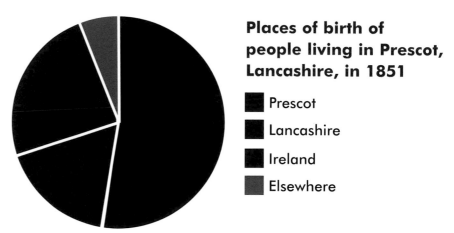

Places of birth of people living in Prescot, Lancashire, in 1851

- ■ Prescot
- ■ Lancashire
- ■ Ireland
- ■ Elsewhere

▲ The census returns for Prescot show that over half of the people living there in 1851 had been born there. Surprisingly, nearly a quarter had been born in another country. Which was it?

Jobs

Ways of working changed greatly during Victorian times. At first, crafts such as pottery, weaving and watchmaking were done by hand at home, or in small workshops. As it became cheaper to mass produce goods in factories, skilled crafts died out.

◀ *Prescot had many watchmakers' shops like this one, photographed in 1893. The long windows gave the watchmaker lots of light to work by.*

▼ *What were the most common jobs in Prescot in 1851? How did this change?*

Occupations of men and boys in Prescot			
	1851	**1861**	**1871**
Bricklayer	49	30	36
Carter	25	28	16
Coalminer	139	44	57
Farm worker	315	149	85
General labourer	246	125	286
Pottery worker	37	8	9
Schoolmaster	3	5	6
Shoemaker	73	52	37
Watchmaker	285	224	204

Occupations of women and girls in Prescot			
	1851	**1861**	**1871**
Charwoman	36	21	26
Dressmaker	63	35	34
Farm worker	67	30	20
Hawker	58	17	1
Laundress	27	15	12
Nurse	18	11	15
Schoolmistress	11	9	14
Servant	211	168	181
Weaver	69	1	0

▼ *These people worked at the Prescot laundry in about 1900.*

Census on-line

Go to www.bbc.co.uk/history/trail and follow the Local History trail to 'census activity'. See what you can find out about the Garthwaites and Coopers, two families living in Coundon, County Durham, in 1851.

Making tracks

Travelling was not easy at the beginning of Victoria's reign. Roads were little more than mud tracks. People walked or used horses for short journeys. Long-distance travel was by stagecoach, and this was slow and expensive. For example, the journey from Somerset to London took two days and cost more than most people earned in a month. Rivers and canals were used to transport goods. Barges could take weeks to reach their destination.

Railway mania

The coming of the railways transformed life in Victorian Britain. In the 1840s 'railway mania' swept the nation. By 1900 a network of railway tracks criss-crossed the country.

Some people were fiercely opposed to the railway building. Canal owners were afraid they would lose business. Local landowners objected to the railway passing through their estates.

Look for evidence showing how people in your locality felt at the time. Is the station built on the edge of town or in the centre? People were sometimes afraid that the railway would bring in undesirable people.

The Pleasures of the Rail-Road. — Caught in the Railway!

▲ At the opening of the first passenger railway in 1830, William Huskisson was knocked down and killed. What did the artist of this cartoon think about the railways?

In the opinion of this meeting a Railway furnishing the most direct communication with London and the Manufacturing and Coal districts having a station at Hitchin would offer many advantages to the Town and Neighbourhood and deserves the support of the inhabitants.

▲ From this report of a meeting in 1844, were people at Hitchin in favour of the railway or not?

15 July 1837

My dear Jane

Thomas had tickets to go with a number of others in the new Steam Carriages on the new Rail Road. It is only finished for 35 miles... I took them to the place of starting, which will be a fine thing when finished. It is at the back of Euston Square...

We waited an hour [for their return] in a fidget at the delay, when at last we saw them advancing rapidly towards us. The first carriage passed, the rest following, all being fastened together, when to my astonishment the first carriage, after a violent concussion which broke down a parapet wall, stood all but on end... It appears that the accident was caused by the engineer not having calculated the additional impetus given by the weight of so many people...

Julia says the feeling of the rapid motion was delightful. The disagreeable part was passing a tunnel, being 5 minutes in utter darkness, and the smell of oil which annoyed her all through. When this rail road is complete people may reach Liverpool in about 8 hours!!...

Your loving sister,

Isobelle

◄ What clues to the benefits of the railway are there in Isobelle's letter to her sister Jane? What disadvantages does she mention?

▼ Euston Station, described in Isobelle's letter, was the first railway station in London. It was opened on 20 July 1837, so Thomas and Julia were on a trial trip.

Train times

How long do you think it takes to get from London to Liverpool by train today? You can find out if you are right by going to www.nationalrail.co.uk.

How did the railway affect our area?

Look for clues to changes in your local area that were caused by the railways. For example, new bridges carried railway lines over roads and rivers. Tunnels had to be blasted through hills, and new roads were built to link to railways.

New buildings

Stations were built alongside the tracks, and houses were put up for railway workers. Is there a Railway Street in your town? Hotels and inns for tired and thirsty travellers sprang up near stations.

▼ Workers on the Clifton Suspension Bridge, near Bristol, in 1864. Is there a railway bridge or viaduct in your area? Many required great feats of engineering that had never been tried before.

▼ Stafford railway station (on the left) was built in 1862. The Station Hotel, on the right, opened in 1866. It had a coffee room for ladies and a billiard room for men.

Pub spotting!

Look out for pub signs that have a connection with the railway. See how many different signs you can collect that have a link with the life and times of Queen Victoria.

Industry

Factories moved to be near stations, as companies took advantage of the railways to transport their products. Faster and cheaper, the railways led to the decline of canals and stagecoaches.

▶ *Allsopp's Brewery, Burton on Trent, was built with its own entrance to the Great Northern Railway Station, so that barrels could be put straight onto trains.*

Transport

Trade directories can show the effect on your local area. Compare the extracts for Maldon in 1839 and 1878. What three types of transport are there in 1839?

Directory.   MALDON, &c.   **Essex.**

COACHES,
FROM THE KING'S HEAD, MALDON.
To LONDON, the *Telegraph*, every Monday, Wednesday, and Friday morning, at ten, and another *Coach* every Monday morning at five, and every other morning (Sunday excepted) at six ; both go thro' Chelmsford, Ingatestone, Brentwood, and Romford.
To BURNHAM, the *Telegraph*, every Tuesday, Thursday, and Saturday afternoon, at five.

CARRIERS.
To LONDON, George French's *Van*, from his office, every Friday at twelve—and Sorrell's *Waggon*, from the Swan Inn, every Tuesday and Friday afternoon.
To BRADWELL, William Creasey, from the Swan Inn, every Monday, Thursday and Saturday afternoon at three
To BURNHAM, William Keys, from the Swan Inn, every Monday, Thursday, and Saturday.

To COLCHESTER, Wm. Keys, from the Swan Inn, every Wednesday and Saturday morning
To TOLLESBURY, Banyard, from the Swan Inn, every Monday, Thursday, and Saturday.
To WITHAM, Agar's *Van*, from the Ship Inn, daily.

CONVEYANCE BY WATER.
To LONDON, John Payne & John Sadd and Son, every Saturday.

---

166   NALDON.   **ESSEX.**   [POST OFFICE

SCHOOLS.
ree (Ralph Breeder's), Market hill, Rev. Thomas Layton Pearson, B.A. master
ritish, Market hill, Frederick William Moss, master ; Miss E. de la Mare, mistress
ational, London road, William Dines, master ; Miss Emily Palmer, mistress
ritish (Infant), High street, Miss Kate French, mistress
. Mary's (Infant), Mill rd. Miss Mary Barnwell, mistress

NEWSPAPER.
aldon Express, High street, Richard Poole, publisher

RAILWAY.
reat Eastern (Braintree, Witham & Maldon Branch), Frederick Blythe, station master ; Mrs. Hickford, agent nnibuses to the Railway station to meet each train, from Blue Boar & King's Head hotels

CARRIERS.
BRADWELL—Alfred Gladwell, monday, wednesday & friday
BURNHAM—David Cross, from 'Swan,' tuesday, thursday & sat.; Charles Withams, from 'Swan,' mon. wed. & fri
CHELMSFORD—Chas. Holmes, from his house, every friday
COLCHESTER—Charles Holmes, from his own house, sat
LONDON—Chas. Wm. Burrells, from his own house, High st. tues. & thur. to 'Saracen's Head,' Aldgate, London
MUNDON, LATCHINGDON, ALTHORNE, & OSTEND—David Cross, from 'Swan,' tuesday, thursday & saturday
PURLEIGH—Joseph Brand, from 'White Horse,' tues. & sat
STEEPLE—Walter Bacon, from 'Swan,' tues. thurs. & sat
SOUTHMINSTER, LATCHINGDON & ALTHORNE—Joseph Livermore, from 'Swan,' daily, sunday excepted
TILLINGHAM, MUNDON & MAYLAND—Walter Bacon, from 'Swan,' tuesday, thursday & saturday
WITHAM—Sayers, from 'Swan,' tuesday, thursday & sat
Mail cart to Burnham & Southminster, daily

What two types of transport are there in 1878? What has changed?

At the end of Victoria's reign, horse and cart was still the most common form of transport. Although the first cars appeared in the 1890s, there were just 1,500 in the whole of Britain in 1901. How many do you think there are today?

Buying and selling

Where do we buy our goods? You might say 'from shops' or even 'on the Internet'. Today we are seeing a revolution in how we buy and sell. There were great changes in Victorian times too.

Markets

At first, when most people lived in the country, markets and fairs were the main places for buying and selling. People sold things that they had made or grown themselves. Markets were usually held once or twice a week.

As towns and industries developed, the people who sold goods were no longer the people who had made them. There were many more goods for sale. Markets and fairs could not cope with people's demands.

▲ *Stafford market square in 1841. A trip to market was a weekly highlight for people living in the surrounding villages. Does your town have a market place?*

Shops

Mass-produced factory goods began to be sold in shops. As fewer people grew their own food, there was a demand for fresh milk and vegetables each day. If you do a survey of a local shopping street in Victorian times, you will find that most of the shops were food shops. It is interesting to compare the type of shops in Victorian times with those in your high street today.

◄ *Look at the meat hanging outside this butcher's shop at Little Haywood, Staffordshire, about 1900.*

HARROW ROAD—continued.
328 & 261 Swift Richard, fruiterer
330 & 548 Greenfield Israel, confectioner
332 &334 London&County Banking Co. Lim. ; Alfred Thos. Roantree, manager
—*Amberley rd.*
336 .Browning Wm., color maker
338 Ollin Wm.,cocoa rms.
340 Warren Francis Wm. & Co., chemists
340 Warren Francis W. & Co., horse & cattle medicine manufactrs
340 Dudley F. & Co., artificial teeth mfrs.
342 Lawrence HenryHayman, draper
344 *Ralphs Stores,*grocrs.
346, 348 & 350 Harvey & Thompson Limited, pawnbrokers
Pillar Letter Box
—*Sutherland avenue*
352 & 354 Rapson Chas., grocer
352 Hunt Mrs. Elizabeth, dressmaker
356 & 358 Darnton Frdk., butcher & cheesemonger
360 Bernard Henry Alexis, baker
—*Marylands rd.*
362 *The Neeld Arms,* Omar Hall
364 .FitzGerald Rbt.,M.D., surgeon
364 Pode Joseph Kirk
366 Powell& Co.,tbccnsts.
366 Parker Mrs. Martha, dentist
368 Lazarus David,clothr.
370 Kavanagh JohnLim., bootmakers
372 Lyon Harold, chemist
374 Lawrance Walter Edward, draper
376 Moore Thomas Treby & Co., mantle mas.
78 Bert Thomas, bootma.

380, 382 & 384 Perring & Co., house furnishrs.
386 Jones Rowland John, dairy
388 Pearce & Co., grocers
390 Mutton William, mantle warehouse
392 Scully James, draper
394 Smith Arthur, china warehouse
396 & 414 Anness Henry, pork butcher
398 Brine W. T., toy & fancy dealer
398 Villiers Portrait Co.
400 Bonner Oswald, ironmonger
402 Lipton Limited, tea & provision merchants
404 & 496 *Metropolitan Boot Co.*
406 Gwyer Thomas, lamp warehouse
408 Cole Henry, funeral furnisher
410 Amies&Sons,bootmas.
412 Phillippo Geo., hosier
414 & 396 Anness Henry, provision merchant
—*Chippenham rd.*
416 Scott Crosbie Fenton
416 London & South Western Bank Lim.; John Leaver Cartwright, manager
418 Fleming, Reid & Co. Limited, wool stores
420 Piper'sLimited,grocrs
420 **MICKLEBURGH CHARLES,** electrical engineer ; specialist in illuminations
122 Berry Fredk.,fruiterer
424 Rapkin Wm., butcher
426 Sumpter Geo. Edwd.
430 Jackson Thomas Edmund, draper
432 Talbert Peter, china dealer
434 Robinson Brothers, clothiers
436 Bernard Henry Alexis, baker
—*Woodfield cres.*
438 .Bernard Henry Alexis, grocer ; post office

440 Jackson RichardWm., watchmaker
442 & 444 WebsterHenry, sewing machine mkr
446 Kates Wm., butcher
450 Ruersch Miss Adelaide, fancy repos.
452 Cope Bros.,hosiers &c.
454 Harris William, tailor
456 Smith Alfred John & Co. Lim., wine mers.
458 Cooper& Co. tea mers.
460 MudgeJohn,carpentr
462 Hockey Wm. confr.
464 *The Elephant & Castle,* Newbery & Tratt
—*Chippenham mews*
466 Redfearn Sml.George, pawnbroker
468 LevellAlbert George, dining rooms
470 & 472 Lilley & Skinner Lim., bootmakers
474 Flood James & Sons, auctioneers
478 **NATIONAL BANK LIM. (THE)** ; Wm. Hodge Bishop,mngr.
—*Elgin avenue*
—*Walterton rd.*
—*Fernhead rd.*
Pillar Letter Box
480 & 482 Alexander Isaac, tailor
480 British Workmen's & General Assurance Co.Limited(William Miles, supt.) (district office)
480 Hicks Alfred, hairdresser
482 Macdonald Manufacturing Co. Lim., artificial teeth mnfrs
484, 486 & 488 McGarrick Chas.& Son, drapers
488 & 484 McGarrick Chas.& Son, drapers
490 Davies D. & Sons, dairymen
492 Layton &Co.,butchers
494 John & James,tea dlrs
496 & 404 *Metropolitan Boot Co.*
498 Journet Robert Wm. stationer

◀ *You can use street directories to find out about local shops and businesses. Who was the shopkeeper at 438 Harrow Road, Paddington? What type of shop was it?*

Which shop?

Today, if beef, broccoli and bread are on your shopping list, you can find them all in one shop – the supermarket. In Victorian times, which three shops would you need to go to? How many types of food shop can you think of? Use the street directory here to help you make a list.

▶ *Here is Harrow Road in about 1900. As competition grew, shopkeepers began to advertise their goods. Many painted signs on the walls of their shops. Sometimes you can still see traces of these painted signs.*

Looking at public buildings

As towns and cities grew and flourished, they liked to show off their wealth with grand buildings. The Victorians' favourite styles of architecture were Classical and Gothic. Classical was based on Greek and Roman temples, which had columns and domes. Can you find a Classical-style building on these pages? Gothic-style buildings look like medieval or fairytale castles. Look out for pointed turrets and narrow, arched windows.

▶ *In which style was Berkhamsted town hall built, in 1859?*

◀ *In Birmingham wealth from the city's industries was used to build the Council House (left), Chamberlain Memorial and Town Hall.*

Schools, libraries and museums

Education was important to the Victorians. Look out for 'National School' or 'British School' on the outside of a building. These were church schools, and most date from the beginning of Victoria's reign. In the 1880s it became compulsory for children to go to school. Many board schools were built, mainly in towns. They are often very tall and look quite forbidding.

Libraries and museums were opened in imposing city-centre buildings. The first public library opened in Westminster in 1857.

Care of the poor

The Victorians made great efforts to fight disease and improve hygiene. New hospitals gave free care to the poor. In the late 1840s, public baths opened where people could wash themselves and their clothes. Almshouses and workhouses were built for the old and poor. Look for Victorian buildings like these in your locality.

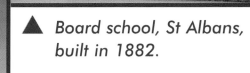

▲ Board school, St Albans, built in 1882.

◄ As towns expanded, new churches were built. Which style was used for this one? A religious census taken in 1851 shows that 60% of people went to church.

▼ New baths and wash houses for the parish of St Pancras, Tottenham Court Road, London, 1877.

What is a workhouse?

Go to www.workhouses.org.uk to find the answer. Follow the links to explore a workhouse in your area.

Public health

There was a darker side to life in Victorian towns and cities. Behind the grand public buildings there were often crowded courts of squalid housing where people had no access to clean water. For toilets, people had a privy – a shed with a wooden seat over a bucket or a hole in the ground. Streets were never cleaned, and diseases like typhoid and cholera brought fear and death.

▲ *These children live in a court. On the left is a privy.*

King Cholera

Privies overflowed into the ground, leaked into wells and polluted the water. When people drank the water, it made them ill.

Cholera was known as 'King Cholera' because no one seemed able to stop it. You might find evidence of a cholera epidemic in your area. For example, 200 cholera victims are buried at the Cefn Golau Cholera Cemetery near Tredegar.

◀ *This parish register shows who died from cholera. What do you notice about the ages?*

Board of Health

In 1848 a Board of Health was set up to investigate why so many people were dying of disease. The chairman of the Board was Edwin Chadwick. He sent health inspectors all over Britain.

Average age of death in 1842				
	Manchester	Liverpool	Leeds	Rutland
Gentlemen	38	35	44	52
Tradesmen	20	26	27	41
Labourers	17	15	19	39

◀ *Was it healthier to live in a town, like Manchester, Liverpool or Leeds, or in a country place like Rutland? Did it make a difference if you were rich or poor?*

These are extracts from the inspectors' reports:

- Nine houses without a privy, excreta and all refuse being thrown into an open pit.

- House slops thrown into the main road and public footway, which is very offensive to passers by.

- Twenty houses (occupied by 84 persons) with four privies standing over the river above the waterworks.

Thanks to Edwin Chadwick's work, the first Public Health Act was passed and towns began to improve. By 1901 there were street cleaners, underground sewers and clean water. We take all these for granted today.

▼ *Emptying outdoor privies in Walsall, about 1900, to stop them overflowing.*

◀ *In 1866, a cholera epidemic in London was traced to a water pump where people collected water to use at home. Find 'King Cholera' in this cartoon from the time.*

Water we use

List all the ways you use water at home. Estimate how many litres your family uses in one day. How many jugs would it take to collect that amount from a street water pump?

House detectives

In 1876 an Act of Parliament gave local councils more power to improve their towns. They began to demolish courts and back-to-back houses. Philanthropic societies, such as the Peabody Trust, helped build better housing for the poor.

Terraces

Houses for workers were built in rows. The houses were joined together to save space but had gardens at the back. Each row was called a terrace.

Suburban villas

As families became better off, they could move out of town centres. Their work was still in the town, so they needed to live nearby. New areas of better housing began to develop around the edges of towns. These are called suburbs. Many people live in suburbs today.

In the spacious suburbs, new houses for the middle class were called villas. These were semi-detached, or detached for the more wealthy.

▲ *Railway Terrace, Machynlleth. These houses have bay windows. Very fashionable in Victorian times, windows like this are a clue to when the street was built.*

◀ *A semi-detached villa in St Albans. The kitchen is below ground. A family living in a villa like this could afford a maid of all work.*

How to identify Victorian houses

Classical and Gothic styles of architecture were used for Victorian houses, as well as for public buildings. For example, notice the narrow, pointed windows in the St Albans villa.

Look out for these special features, which will help you to identify houses built in Victorian times:

- bay windows
- decorated bargeboards
- finials
- earthenware chimney pots
- decorated brickwork.

Make a map

Draw a map of your local area. Try to date when a street was built by looking at the houses. Colour in the streets using three different colours. Use one for pre-Victorian building, one for Victorian streets, and one for streets built after Victorian times. Use your map to explain how your area developed.

Victorian houses had more fireplaces because coal was cheap. This meant they had lots of chimneys. Chimney pots became more decorative as factories could produce different designs.

◀ *A decorated bargeboard, with a finial where the boards meet at the top. Can you see the finials on the roofs of Railway Terrace?*

▲▶ *Look for patterns made from coloured bricks. Bricks made in different parts of the country are red, yellow or grey, depending on the colour of the local clay. The new railways made it possible to transport bricks around the country and builders took advantage of this.*

Clues to 'the Age of Iron'

If you walk around your town, you may be surprised how much evidence you can find of life in Victorian times. You just have to keep your eyes open.

Street names

Look out for street names that give a clue to when the houses were built. Victorian signs were made of cast iron. Some were on blue enamel. Modern name plates use a lighter metal.

▲
◄ *Victoria and Albert were very popular names in Queen Victoria's reign. Victoria's husband was Prince Albert.*

◄ *Gladstone was a Victorian prime minister.*

◄ *Is there an Alma, Inkerman or Sebastopol Road in your town? These are people and events connected with the Crimean War.*

▲ *You might find the names Ladysmith, Kimberley or Mafeking. These commemorate the Boer War.*

Street furniture

The Victorian period is sometimes called 'the Age of Iron'. Cast iron was used to make pillar boxes (first put up in 1852), lamp posts, coal hole covers and even boot scrapers. You can still find these today, but they are fast disappearing.

◄ *A boot scraper at the door was essential when horses were the main form of transport. Can you picture what the roads were like?*

◀ *Coal was used for all heating and cooking in Victorian houses. It was delivered through holes in the pavement, straight into the cellars. Coal hole covers often have symmetrical designs, and can be dated by linking the maker's name with trade directories.*

Street lighting

In early Victorian times streets were lit by gas. Electricity was first used in London in 1879, but in most places it was much later.

▶ *Notice the 'arms' near the top of this Victorian lamp post. This was where the lamplighter rested his ladder. He had to light the gas lamps every evening, and put them out every morning.*

◀ *This pillar box in Cambridge is one of the oldest in Britain. It dates from 1856. The initials 'VR' stand for 'Victoria Regina' which is Latin for Queen Victoria. Can you guess what 'ER II' on modern post boxes stands for?*

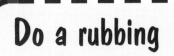

Do a rubbing

Look out for street furniture where you live. Do a rubbing of a pattern on a coal hole cover, the initials on a pillar box, or another decorative cast iron feature. Experiment with different types of paper and drawing materials. Wax crayons work well.

COMMON

23

Written in stone

The Victorians loved to celebrate. You can find many plaques and memorials which tell about the lives of local people.

▼ *This beautiful plaque on the wall of the London Orphan Asylum (1871) shows it was a place of safety for children who had no parents. There were separate schools for boys and girls.*

Design a memorial

Choose an event or person connected with your local area today. Why would it be important to remember them? What do you want to make people think about? What words and images will you use? Make a sketch of your design.

Queen Victoria

In 1897 Queen Victoria had reigned for 60 years. Her Diamond Jubilee was celebrated in many ways. People were very proud of their queen, and all that had been achieved during her long reign. Parks and recreation grounds were opened. Statues and memorials were erected. You might find one in your town.

▶ *Can you find the date of this plaque? It tells us that Victoria was known as Empress of India as well as Queen of Canada, Australia, the West Indies and several other countries.*

Investigating a churchyard

A good way to find out about life in Victorian times is to look at the gravestones in your local churchyard. Sometimes people's jobs are given. You may be surprised at how many children's graves you find. Many died before their first birthday. You could choose a family and find out more about their lives from the census.

▼ *The Victorians chose more and more elaborate gravestones.*

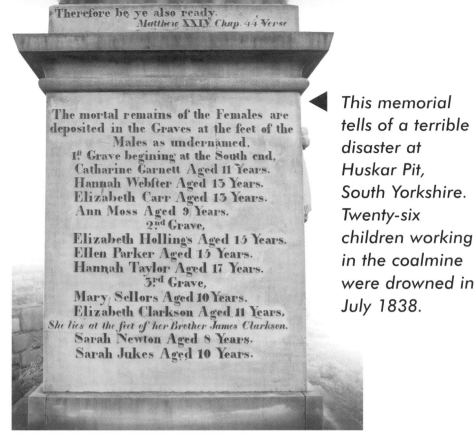

◀ *This memorial tells of a terrible disaster at Huskar Pit, South Yorkshire. Twenty-six children working in the coalmine were drowned in July 1838.*

▼ *James Hanley was killed in 1855 in an accident at an iron foundry. You might find a newspaper report for more details of a local accident like this.*

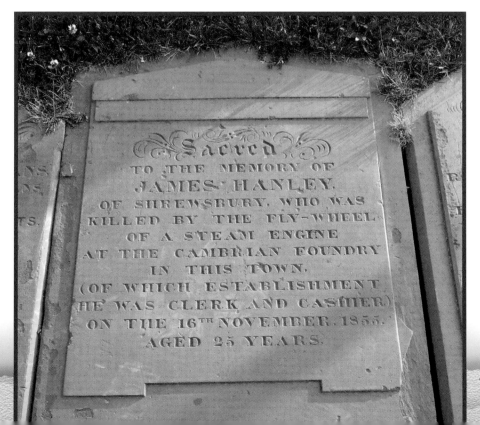

Mapping the changes

You can see an amazing snapshot of your local area by looking at a map. Maps show what was on the ground at a particular time. Put snapshots from different dates together, and you can see how your locality changed.

OS maps

Start with the earliest (large-scale) Ordnance Survey (OS) map of your area. These began in the 1860s. As each county was mapped in turn, some areas do not have detailed printed maps until the 1880s. A second edition was begun in the 1890s.

Compare the two OS maps on this page to see how one part of Birmingham changed in late Victorian times. Can you find the tree from which Three Shires Oak Road took its name? Find a clue on page 4 to see what happened to the tree.

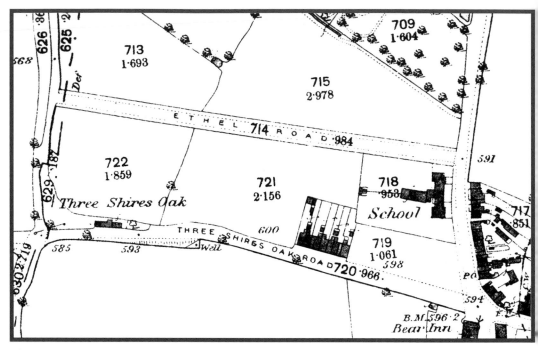

▲ The first OS map of Three Shires Oak Road, Birmingham, was printed in 1886.

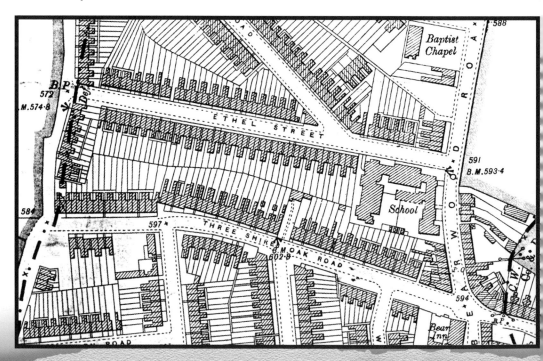

► The second edition of the map was printed in 1904. What has changed since 1886?

Tithe maps

To find out what your area was like at the beginning of Queen Victoria's reign, you can use a tithe map. These were drawn by hand in the late 1830s or 1840s.

Compare the two maps of Park Street on this page to see how this locality changed during Victorian times. Can you find any of the following which are there in 1874 but not in 1838?

- Railway
- School
- Hospital
- Chapel
- Road
- Bridge
- House

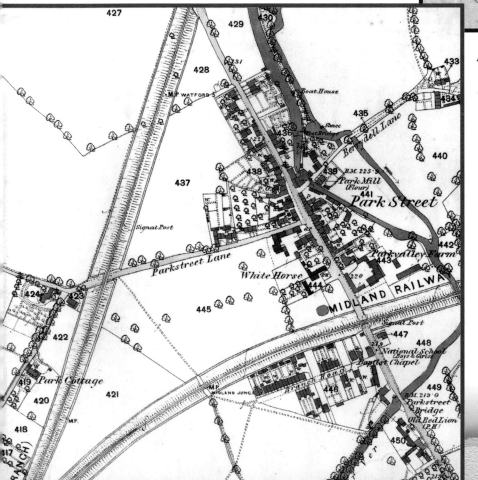

▲ *This tithe map shows Park Street in 1838.*

◄ *What changes had taken place by 1874, when this OS map was printed?*

Timeline

Use a digital camera to take photos of buildings, street furniture, memorials, etc. Put them in order of date between 1837 and 1901. Import them into your computer, and create a virtual trip through time to see how your locality changed.

Glossary

agricultural labourer   a farm worker.

almshouse   a house for the poor, paid for by charity.

back-to-back houses   cheap houses for the poor, joined together at the sides and back. With windows only at the front, the houses had little light or ventilation.

barge   a long, flat-bottomed boat for carrying goods on canals. In Victorian times barges were pulled by horses, walking along a tow-path by the canal.

bargeboards   wooden boards attached to the arches of roofs or doorways. Quite plain at first, they became more decorated, especially in the 1860s.

bay window   a window shaped like a box; a fashionable style in Victorian houses, instead of curved 'bow windows'.

Board of Health   a committee set up by Parliament in 1848 to improve public health.

board schools   state schools set up after Forster's Education Act of 1870 where there were not enough schools already.

Boer War   fought by Britain (1899-1902) against the Boers, Dutch settlers in South Africa.

cast iron   made by pouring a mixture of molten iron and carbon into a mould. This was a cheap way of mass producing metal objects.

census   a count of people living in a country. In Britain it has been taken every 10 years since 1801 (except 1941).

census enumerator   a person who visits houses at the time of a census and records information about the people there.

charwoman   a woman who worked as a cleaner, especially scrubbing floors.

cholera   a disease caused by drinking polluted water.

church schools   schools set up by churches for children from ordinary working families. National Schools were set up by the Church of England and British Schools by non-conformist churches.

court   houses grouped around a small enclosed yard, reached from the street through a narrow passageway.

Crimean War   war fought near the Black Sea in 1853-56, by Britain, France, Sardinia and Turkey against Russia.

earthenware   made of fired clay.

enamel   a hard, glossy coating which can be used on metal surfaces for decoration.

epidemic   a widespread outbreak of a disease.

famine   an extreme shortage of food, leading to starvation.

finial   a decorative point at the top of gables.

foundry   a workshop for casting metal.

hawker   a person who travels around selling goods.

hygiene   clean and healthy practices.

industry   factories using machines to produce more goods to sell.

Jubilee   an anniversary of a monarch's reign. Victoria's Golden (1887) and Diamond (1897) Jubilees were marked with great outpourings of public affection.

laundress	a woman who does washing and ironing for people.
locality	a place where you live.
maid of all work	a female servant who did everything that, in richer houses, would be done by a cook, kitchen maid and parlour maid.
mania	extreme enthusiasm. When railways were invented, many people became so excited that they started to build railway lines all over the country.
mass produce	to make a lot of goods quickly and cheaply, using machines in factories.
medical officer	a person appointed to look after people's health. Victorian medical officers produced reports about living conditions in their local area.
memorial	a statue, or other object, put up in memory of a person or event.
Ordnance Survey	an army department which produced the first printed maps in 1800, at a scale of one inch to the mile. In the 1850s it produced some town plans (50 inches to the mile) and then large-scale maps (25 inches to the mile).
Orphan Asylum	a home for children whose parents have died.
parish	a local area with its own church. In Victorian times the people of each parish decided what should be spent on road repairs and on caring for the poor.
parish register	a record of baptisms, marriages and burials, kept by a church, from 1538 to the present day.
philanthropic	wanting to help people, usually by giving money.
pillar box	a public postbox, pillar-shaped and painted red.
plaque	an ornamental tablet fixed to a building in memory of a person or event.
sewers	underground pipes or tunnels for removing sewage (waste from toilets and drains).
squalid	filthy and horrible.
stagecoach	a large, closed, horsedrawn carriage, which travelled between the main towns and cities, changing horses at each stage or stopping place.
street directory	list of streets in a town, with names of people running shops and businesses; started in the 1850s.
suburbs	built-up areas around towns, created as workers moved out of town centres.
terrace	three or more houses joined in a row.
tithe maps	large-scale maps produced for every parish in England and Wales (1836-50). Fields and houses are numbered and listed, showing who owned and lived in each farm or cottage.
trade directory	information about villages and towns in an area, with lists of shops and tradespeople; started in the 1830s.
turret	a small tower.
typhoid	a deadly disease caused by contaminated water.
viaduct	a bridge carrying a railway or road across a valley.
villa	a detached or semi-detached house in the suburbs.
wheelwright	someone who made large wooden wheels for carts.
workhouse	a grim building, like a prison, where the poor had to live in Victorian times. May be part of a hospital today.

For teachers and parents

This book is designed to support and extend the learning objectives of Unit 12 of the QCA History Scheme of Work. It links with Unit 11 and the book *Step-up History: Children in Victorian Times*.

Looking at the history of your local area is an exciting way to bring history alive. The use of the built environment encourages active learning. It can engage all the senses, awakening children to take a fresh look at what they see every day and to ask questions about it.

A visit to the local archives, library or museum will be important in helping children to develop research skills and to understand how to find out about the past. This book introduces a range of primary sources, including census returns, parish registers, gravestones, local newspapers, photographs and maps, and shows how they fit together like a jigsaw to recreate the past in your community.

Children enjoy detective work, which is a key part of a local study. Looking for clues, evaluating the evidence and piecing it together to draw conclusions about the past and how the locality has changed, all develop analytical and enquiry skills. There is scope for differentiation and progression, as individual children can pursue their own line of enquiry, relating for example to one family, house, street or school. Questions should be asked about what has changed, and also why it changed. In looking for causes, changes in the locality should be seen in the wider context of change within Victorian Britain.

Exploring the local heritage can play an important part in developing a sense of identity and community. Oral history, using memories of older members of the community, can help to develop a sense of chronology and link the Victorian period to life today.

There are opportunities for cross-curricular work, particularly in literacy, mathematics, geography, science, religious education, citizenship, art and design. ICT has an important role, supporting children's learning, and links well with work on census returns.

SUGGESTED FURTHER ACTIVITIES

Pages 4 – 5 Finding out about the Victorians

With the children, make a list of sources we can use to find out about the past. Decide which are primary sources (those made at the time, e.g. census) and which are secondary sources (those written later, e.g. Internet). Discuss which are more reliable and why.

Ask children to take a photograph of their school, street or family and then to draw a picture of the same scene. What differences do they notice? What are the advantages and disadvantages of photographs and of drawings as evidence? The children should imagine they are in the future, and use the pictures they have made to write about life in the early 21st century.

Pages 6 – 7 Who lived here?

Can the children find any Victorian photos of their families? Try using the census to date old photographs. Facsimile copies of the 1851-1901 census for England and Wales can be downloaded and printed from www.ancestry.co.uk. You pay to use this site, but it is free in some public libraries. For Scotland see www.scotlandspeople.gov.uk.

The census page on page 6 shows the Dye family. (There is more about James Dye in *Step-up History: Children in Victorian Times*.) Children could use the census to draw a family tree of the Dye family. In 1851 Mary Dye said she was born in Hertford. In 1861 she said she was born in Ireland, and in 1871 she said she was born 'aboard a ship'. Where do the children think Mary was born? Use this to discuss why information in the census may not be true. It depends what people told the enumerator at the time.

Discuss why we take a census today (e.g. to know how many schools or hospitals to build).

Pages 8 – 9 Doing a people count

Children could choose a column from one of the tables of occupations in Prescot and present it as a graph or pie chart. Discuss with them how the occupations could be grouped into larger categories: e.g. farming, service, crafts, professional, manual.

Using copies of census returns, ask the children to formulate a research question relating to family size, jobs, birthplaces, etc. Discuss what information to collect and how to organise it. Use ICT to present.

Compare census returns for the same street in different years. Are any of the same families still living there? Have occupations changed?

Invite someone to come and speak to the class about moving in to the community, or about a local craft that has disappeared.

Pages 10 – 11 Making tracks

Imagining being farmers, against the coming of the railway, children could explain their objections in a letter to the local paper. Or they could design a poster encouraging people to visit the seaside by train.

Have a class debate about the advantages and disadvantages of railway travel today. How have railway services improved? How have they declined? Should we have more or fewer railways today?

Pages 12 – 13 How did the railway affect our area?

Use *Dombey and Son* (chapters 6 and 15) for some powerful descriptive writing. You could also discuss how novels can be used as historical evidence. Charles Dickens had mixed views about the railway. Can the children find clues to this in his writing?

To find out more about the development of the railways, children could go to www.makingthemodernworld.org.uk and select 'Age of the Engineer' from the Stories Timeline.

Pages 14 – 15 Buying and selling
Encourage the children to look for mosaic floors in shop doorways. The Victorians used small coloured tiles to make a pattern, often with the name of the shopkeeper in the middle. Children could design their own mosaic pattern, perhaps putting their name in the middle.

Use advertisements in a Victorian newspaper to look at life at the time. Talk about whether their claims would be believed today. Are any of the products still sold and advertised?

Pages 16 – 17 Looking at public buildings
Encourage the children to find out more about a public building in your area. When was it built? What style of architecture is it in? Is it still used for its original purpose? If your school is Victorian, look for evidence of original features, e.g. central hall, separate boys' and girls' entrances, outside toilets.

Children could make a model of a local Victorian building. Discuss how to work out the height of the building and the scale to use.

Pages 18 – 19 Public health
Discuss what enables us to lead healthy lives today. The children could find out about local services, e.g. waste disposal, water supply, sewage, street cleaning. Then they could imagine if these did not exist.

Hold a mock election for your local council. Candidates must say how they will spend the council tax collected and why. What new services would the children vote for?

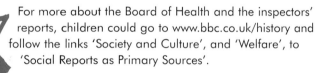

For more about the Board of Health and the inspectors' reports, children could go to www.bbc.co.uk/history and follow the links 'Society and Culture', and 'Welfare', to 'Social Reports as Primary Sources'.

Pages 20 – 21 House detectives
Children could take a walk to make sketches of different designs of one particular feature, e.g. windows or chimneys. The sketches could be used to produce a class artwork.

Ask the children to draw their own architectural design for a house. What decorative features will they use? What building materials? They should give their architectural style an appropriate name.

The Victorians loved using coloured glass. Children could make their own 'stained glass window' from black sugar paper and coloured tissue paper or cellophane. The sugar paper 'frame' can be whatever shape they like, with lots of interesting shapes inside. Stick or hang the finished windows in front of a clear glass window.

Pages 22 – 23 Clues to 'the Age of Iron'
Children could use a digital camera to record as many examples of street furniture as they can, for a class display.

Talk about materials used for street furniture today, e.g. plastic, stainless steel, concrete. You could ask children to find one item of street furniture made from each of these, at www.furnitubes.com. What are the advantages and disadvantages of each material?

Pages 24 – 25 Written in stone
To learn how Victoria's Diamond Jubilee was celebrated in your locality, look for photographs, school log books and local papers.

Link to citizenship by discussing how attitudes to the British Empire have changed and why. What happened to the countries mentioned on the plaque? The Indian 'Mutiny' (1857) is today better known as the Indian 'Uprising'. Discuss how language affects meaning.

Gravestones can be used to draw family trees or to make a graph of the most popular first names of people who died in Victorian times.

Help the children to investigate mortality statistics in your area. The average age of death was 30 in 1800, 41 in 1850 and 50 in 1900. For poor people in towns it could be much lower.

Pages 26 – 27 Mapping the changes
Children could compare a modern map of their town, village or street with a map of the area in Victorian times. What has changed?

ADDITIONAL RESOURCES
To experience Victorian housing brought to life, recommended visits are the Birmingham back-to-backs (National Trust), Rhyd-y-car mining cottages (Museum of Welsh Life) and Port Sunlight.

To find primary and secondary sources for your local area, including census returns, photographs, maps and directories, contact your local studies library or archives. Ask about resource packs. You can find contact details at www.archon.nationalarchives.gov.uk.

Many archives, museums and libraries are putting images online. Check if any are available for your locality. Some examples are:
www.picturethepast.org.uk (Derbyshire)
www.thegrid.org.uk/learning/hals/victorians.htm (Hertfordshire)
history.knowsley.gov.uk (Lancashire)
www.tengenerations.org.uk (London)
history.powys.org.uk (Powys)
www.scan.org.uk (Scotland)
www.staffspasttrack.org.uk (Staffordshire)
www.gtj.org.uk (Wales)
www.wiltshire.gov.uk/community (Wiltshire)

Historical maps can be downloaded from www.old-maps.co.uk, but for larger-scale maps go to your local library. Directories can be viewed at www.historicaldirectories.org. For the built environment see English Heritage's 'Learning Zone' at www.imagesofengland.org.uk/education.

Index